T0110674

Try It! *More* Math Problems for All

This is not your typical math book.

Try It! More Math Problems for All is the second of three collections of offbeat, open-ended problems designed to make even the most math-averse student excited about working through these challenging yet accessible problems.

These are 25 new, illustrated problems varying in difficulty. They will motivate your students to think creatively on their own and to engage in teamwork. The **Hints and Solutions** section guides you to probe, suggest, and encourage students to explore even their most unusual insights on the way to a solution. And when students solve a problem, you will see and hear their accomplishments.

Perfect for any math classroom, club, after school activity, or coaching session, *Try It!* celebrates not only the destination, but the journey, giving students a chance to think differently, and, above all, have fun!

Can't get enough? Volumes 1 and 3 in the series are also available at Routledge.com.

Optional Student Workbook Packs

In addition to this teachers' guide, companion student workbooks are available in packs of ten. The student workbooks feature ample room for student responses and notes, make reviewing and providing feedback on student work easy, provide students with a quick reference to use during discussions, and they save time – there is no need to reproduce student handouts.

Jerry Kaplan is Professor Emeritus of Mathematics Education at Seton Hall University, where he taught for 28 years. He has written widely on many areas of teaching and learning mathematics, applying research to the practical needs of the mathematics curriculum and classroom, and is a strong advocate for including quality problems as an integral part of good math instruction.

Try It! *More* Math Problems for All

Jerry Kaplan

Illustrated by Ysemay Dercon

Routledge
Taylor & Francis Group

NEW YORK AND LONDON

Designed cover image: Ysemay Dercon

First published 2024
by Routledge
605 Third Avenue, New York, NY 10158

and by Routledge
4 Park Square, Milton Park, Abingdon, Oxon, OX14 4RN

Routledge is an imprint of the Taylor & Francis Group, an informa business

ISBN: 978-1-032-52417-7 (hbk)
ISBN: 978-1-032-51569-4 (pbk)
ISBN: 978-1-003-40658-7 (ebk)

DOI: 10.4324/9781003406587

Typeset in Bembo
by Deanta Global Publishing Services, Chennai, India

Contents

Preface

To students everywhere,

Hi, I am Jerry and I have 25 new problems. Find one you like and **TRY IT!** That's right. **TRY IT!** We do not ask too much. Just **TRY IT!**

If you cannot figure it out, leave it alone. Then come back to it. Or try another one. And try some more. Speak to a classmate about it. Take your time. Some kids do not get it for a week. That's okay. This is not a race.

After a while, ask for help. A **hint**. Maybe another **hint?**

Try five different problems. Did it get any easier? Soon, you will have a favorite problem. Do not give up.

As a teacher, I spent years challenging students with problems. It started when I was a first-grade teacher. I asked my 19 students to figure out who was the oldest in the class. That took a month to figure out because first all the kids had to find out their exact dates of birth. Then we had to learn new stuff about calendars, years, months, weeks, and days. And finally, we wrote down the names of the oldest and youngest in the class with their birth dates. Later, we made a poster listing the whole class from youngest to oldest. I'll never forget the chatter from the kids about where they were on that list! Very exciting for all. And more: we made lists showing who was born in January, February, March, and so forth. I think I did more teaching in those four weeks than in any other four weeks of my teaching career!

From that experience I realized I wanted to use problem solving in all my classes. I did it later when I taught high school, and continued when I taught in college. Not only did my students have fun and a chance to work together, but students went home and tried our problems on family and friends. And came back to tell stories about all the trouble other folks had solving our problems!

What did you learn about how to solve problems?

First, take your time. **TRY IT!** and **TRY IT!** again. If you need a **hint**, ask for it. Or, try another problem. Another **hint?** Work on two at the same time. Keep thinking. After a while, you will learn you are better at solving problems than you thought! And that is a lot to learn.

Try It! Hints and Solutions

To teachers everywhere,

Try It! Hints and Solutions is a companion to **Try It! More Math Problems for All**. This is the second of three in the **Try It!** series. As before, this part of the volume consists of many helpful hints and all the solutions for teachers to use in their classrooms. Beyond classrooms, **Hints and Solutions** is for anyone who takes a crack at the problems.

The problems. The purposes of the problems are to engage and challenge. We want to give you and your students a break from the steady routine of drill and practice found in standard math lessons. But even more important, we want students of all backgrounds (and ages) to have a chance to think and grapple with an array of problems, whether alone or with others.

These problems are different from what you see in schools. They are not connected to the usual lessons or to the yearlong curriculum of any grade. Even more, they are not intended to be inserted at any specific time during the year. They are not aligned to any part of school teachings. Of course, that might be a stretch since with a bit of effort you can find a place and a time to insert a problem here or there in your program. We suggest that you don't. You will lose spontaneity and the purpose of these problems.

When and where. Use them early or late in the school year. Use them on special days. Use them with one or more students. Small groups make sense. But above all give solvers time to think and brainstorm. Take the problems home? No problem. Remember, there is no clock such as "Your deadline is next Wednesday".

Start anywhere in the set. You will find easy and difficult problems next to each other. Encourage students to write their work down on paper. And when a student or a group has a solution, you may want to check it quietly. Eventually, you may want students to present their solutions to the class. Some teachers organize a REVEAL DAY for that purpose.

DOI: 10.4324/9781003406587-1

And for you. Have fun presenting problems to your groups – small, large, young, and old. Here is a chance to prod them forward as your audience starts to shout out solutions. By throwing out hints and clues here and there, you encourage more probing. Do not give it away too soon. And above all have fun. Tease kindly. Play.

Background. We used these problems in courses at colleges and in many workshops with teachers and students from 5th to 12th grades. They are used today in schools by many teachers we know. We've presented them to people of all ages – and we all had fun.

Be surprised. These problems are for all students, the high and low achievers, the quiet and loud ones. You probably know this: sometimes the quietest and/or the lowest performing students will surprise you if you give them a chance. They surprised us, for sure.

The accent is on **TRY IT!**

A Few Tips

We recognize that it is difficult to translate our personal tastes and styles for other teachers. But there are methods that, when timed correctly, will motivate your students, and encourage them to keep trying when solving problems. In the end, persistence by individuals and groups will solve problems and help to understand the "why" behind the solutions.

Here are a few tips on getting students engaged in solving problems.

- Encourage students to "throw out" ideas, that is, to brainstorm and talk to each other.
- Arrange groups so that students solve problems with other students.
- "Other students" can be one or as many as four or five students.
- If several groups are working at the same time, keep an eye on every group.
- Keep all students involved.
- Encourage students to explain to other students.
- Do not offer direct help, only tidbits of assistance.
- Keep encouraging students throughout.
- Groups are not in competition; give different problems to different groups.
- Encourage students to write their ideas on paper; research favors writing things down when problem solving.
- Do not rush problem-solving sessions.

Organization of this Guide

We devote two pages to each problem: A **HINTS** page and a **SOLUTIONS** page. You will find all problems here exactly as you see them in the student workbook.

HINTS: You will find the problem and several hints or prompts on how to get started on the problem.

- Make sure students understand the problem.
- Use these hints only after students understand the problem and had a chance to discuss it within their group.
- Offer hints only after students have made several attempts at solving and seem honestly stuck.
- The longer students struggle with finding a solution, the more they will learn from each other.
- Do not hint too early; that could impede those who are eager to figure things out on their own.
- Suggest that students take a break and come back to the problem later in the day or the next day.

SOLUTIONS: The problem is here again followed by a worked-out solution to the problem and the answer.

1 FINDING A PAIR IN THE DARK

You have 10 red socks and 10 blue socks mixed in a drawer. These socks are all the same except for color. One night you enter the room in pitch darkness and open the drawer to get a pair of socks. What is the smallest number of socks you must pick out of the drawer to insure you have a pair of socks of the same color? Remember you cannot see what you picked.

HINTS

Make a list of possible picks.

Pick #1: R or B
Pick #2: R or B

After 2 picks, here is what is possible:

RR   RB   BR   BB

1 FINDING A PAIR IN THE DARK

You have 10 red socks and 10 blue socks mixed in a drawer. These socks are all the same except for color. One night you enter the room in pitch darkness and open the drawer to get a pair of socks. What is the smallest number of socks you must pick out of the drawer to insure you have a pair of socks of the same color? Remember you cannot see what you picked.

SOLUTION

Make a list of the possible picks.

Pick #1: R or B
Pick #2: R or B

Here is what is possible after 2 picks:

RR   RB   BR   BB

Here is what is possible after 3 picks:

RRR   BRR   RBR   RRB   RBB   BRB   BBR   BBB

Answer: The smallest number of socks you must pick is 3. After three picks you will always have two socks of the same color.

2 PLANTING BUSHES IN A LINE

Ahmed wanted to make an attractive design from the 10 bushes he bought for the front lawn. He was able to plant the 10 identical bushes in 5 lines of 4 bushes each. How can that be done? Show it with a drawing.

HINTS

Line them up in rows.
You can get 2 rows of 5.

Or you can get 5 rows of 2.

What other ways can you line the bushes?

2 PLANTING BUSHES IN A LINE

Ahmed wanted to make an attractive design from the 10 bushes he bought for the front lawn. He was able to plant the 10 identical bushes in 5 lines of 4 bushes each. How can that be done? Show it with a drawing.

SOLUTION

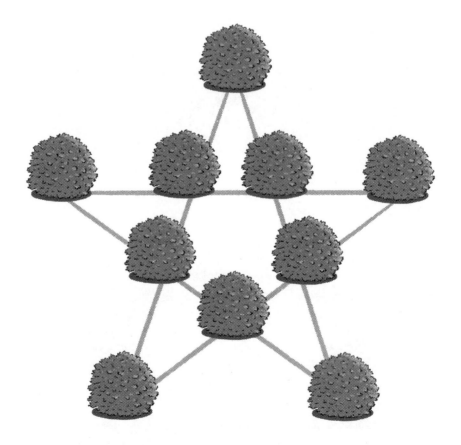

<u>Answer: The bushes form the diagonals of a pentagon.</u>

3 DIVIDING LAND EQUALLY

Carmen owns a large tract of land in the shape of a square.

She wants to divide the land equally among her four sons. She first divides the land into four equal squares and takes one of the squares for herself. How can she divide the remaining land among her four sons, so each gets the same area and the same shape? Draw your answer. Show the area Carmen keeps for herself and the shape of the areas she gives to her sons.

HINTS

Carmen keeps ¼ of the land for herself by cutting the land into four equal squares. She takes one of those squares for herself.

Now you must cut the remaining ¾ of the land, X, Y, and Z, into four pieces, each having the same shape and area. Provide a drawing that shows how to do that.

Carmen's	X
Y	Z

3 DIVIDING LAND EQUALLY

Carmen owns a large tract of land in the shape of a square.

She wants to divide the land equally among her four sons. She first divides the land into four equal squares and takes one of the squares for herself. How can she divide the remaining land among her four sons, so each gets the same area and the same shape? Draw your answer. Show the area Carmen keeps for herself and the shape of the areas she gives to her sons.

SOLUTION

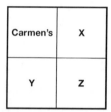

Carmen must divide the combined area of X, Y, and Z into 4 equal areas that have the same shapes. One way to do this is to divide the combined area into 12 equal parts first.

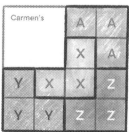

Answer:

Next, now that she has 12 equal parts, she can put 3 of them together 4 times. Finally, she has 4 equal areas. Here they are as the same L shape.

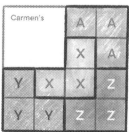

4 CHOOSING ONE FOR ALL

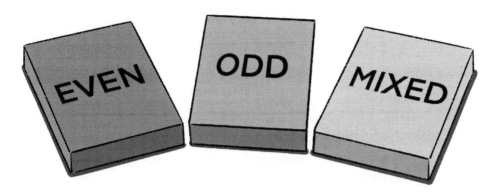

Your friend Wayne shows you three boxes of cards.

Box A: all cards have even numbers.
Box B: all cards have odd numbers.
Box C: cards are mixed – some have even numbers and the rest have odd numbers.

The three boxes have labels on top – EVEN, ODD, MIXED. But the labels are mixed up and not on the right boxes.

How can you choose one card from one box and tell exactly what is in all three boxes? Explain.

HINTS

ODD	EVEN	MIXED

Remember the labels are not correct. The box of even numbers might have the label ODD.

This means if you choose one card from the MIXED box, the cards will be either all even or all odd.

4 CHOOSING ONE FOR ALL

Your friend Wayne shows you three boxes of cards.

Box A: all cards have even numbers.

Box B: all cards have odd numbers.

Box C: cards are mixed – some have even numbers and the rest have odd numbers.

The three boxes have labels on top – EVEN, ODD, MIXED. But the labels are mixed up and not on the right boxes.

How can you choose one card from one box and tell exactly what is in all three boxes? Explain.

SOLUTION

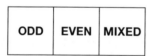

ODD	EVEN	MIXED

Remember the labels are not correct. The box of even numbers might have the label ODD.

This means if you choose one card from the MIXED box, the cards could be all even or all odd.

Pick a card from the MIXED box. Suppose you pick an odd card. Remember, the label is wrong. That means the entire box has <u>odd</u> cards. That means that the other two boxes are mixed cards and even cards.

Which cards are in the box labeled EVEN? The cards cannot be even since the label is wrong. And the cards cannot be odd since we already picked from the box of odd numbers. So, the box with the label EVEN is the box with mixed cards. So, the last box (marked ODD) has the even cards. Here is the summary:

The box marked MIXED has the odd numbers.

The box marked EVEN has mixed numbers.

The box marked ODD has even numbers.

If you picked an even number from the MIXED box, then the box marked MIXED has even cards, the box marked ODD has mixed cards, and the box marked EVEN has odd cards.

Answer: Choose a card from the box labeled MIXED.

5 CONSTRUCTING REVOLUTIONARY EQUATIONS

Use each digit of 1776 once to construct equations. Here is an example equal to 3.

$$6 \div (1 + 7/7) = 3$$

Now use each digit of 1776 once to construct an equation equal to each of these digits: 1, 2, 4, 5, 6, 7, 8, 9.

That means write eight different equations.

_____ = 1   _____ = 6

_____ = 2   _____ = 7

_____ = 4   _____ = 8

_____ = 5   _____ = 9

HINTS

Study the given example: $6 \div (1 + 7/7) = 3$.

Notice how the 7s are used: $7/7 = 1$.

And see how the parentheses are utilized.

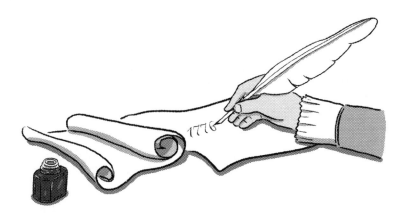

5 CONSTRUCTING REVOLUTIONARY EQUATIONS

Use each digit of 1776 once to construct equations. Here is an example equal to 3.

$$6 \div (1 + 7/7) = 3$$

Now use each digit of 1776 once to construct an equation equal to each of these digits: 1, 2, 4, 5, 6, 7, 8, 9.

That means write 8 different equations.

_____ = 1		_____ = 6
_____ = 2		_____ = 7
_____ = 4		_____ = 8
_____ = 5		_____ = 9

SOLUTIONS

$(7 - 7) \times 6 + 1 = 1$

$(7 + 7) \div (1 + 6) = 2$

$6 - (1 + 7/7) = 4$

$6 - (1 \times 7/7) = 5$

$6 \times 1 \times 7/7 = 6$

$6 + (1 \times 7/7) = 7$

$6 + (1 + 7/7) = 8$

$(7 + 7 + 1) - 6 = 9$

6 ARRIVING AT THE SAME TIME?

You have two clocks in front of you. Clock #1 runs smoothly. Clock #2 also runs smoothly and at the same rate as Clock #1, but the hands move backwards. If they both start at 8 o'clock, when will they show the same time again? Explain.

HINTS

What are the times on the clocks after 1 hour?

Clock #1 _____ Clock #2 _____

What are the times on the clocks after 2 hours?

Clock #1 _____ Clock #2 _____

What are the times on the clocks after 3 hours?

Clock #1 _____ Clock #2 _____

6 ARRIVING AT THE SAME TIME?

You have two clocks in front of you. Clock #1 runs smoothly. Clock #2 also runs smoothly and at the same rate as Clock #1, but the hands move backwards. If they both start at 8 o'clock, when will they show the same time again? Explain.

SOLUTION

What are the times on the clocks after 4 hours?

Clock #1 _____ Clock #2 _____

What are the times on the clocks after 5 hours?

Clock #1 _____ Clock #2 _____

What are the times on the clocks after 6 hours?

Clock #1 _____ Clock #2 _____

Or, the hour hand will rotate back to 8 in 12 hours, so halfway around to 2 in 6 hours.

Answer: After 6 hours, the two clocks will show the same time: 2 o'clock.

7 GETTING TO 50 FIRST

Let's play the Game of 50. You and a friend both start at 0 along the same number line.

Decide who goes first and then take turns. For every turn, players advance by at least one step, but no more than six steps. When it is your turn, say the number of steps you will take. The first person to get to 50 wins.

Figure out a winning strategy.

HINTS

Encourage the Game of 50 in your group.
Repeat several times while thinking of a winning strategy.
Remind players of the rule to take steps from 1 to 6.
Ask: what happens if you land on 40? Do you win or lose?
What happens if you land on 41? Do you win or lose?

7 GETTING TO 50 FIRST

Let's play the Game of 50. You and a friend both start at 0 along the same number line.

Decide who goes first and then take turns. For every turn, players advance by at least one step, but no more than six steps. When it is your turn, say the number of steps you will take. The first person to get to 50 wins.

Figure out a winning strategy.

SOLUTIONS

What happens if you land on 40?
Is it a good strategy to land on 40?
Getting to 40 first is not a good strategy.
Getting to 41 first is also not a good strategy.
Do you see why?
A very good strategy is to get to 43 first. Then it does not matter what move your opponent makes, you will get to 50 first.

Answer: Get to 43 first.

This also means get to 36 first so you can get to 43 first.

8 COUNTING AUTOMOBILES AND MOTORCYCLES

The Parnell family came back from a combined automobile-motorcycle show impressed by all the new models they saw. The brochure said that there were 70 different vehicles on display with a total of 200 wheels. How many were automobiles? How many were motorcycles?

HINTS

How many wheels on an automobile?
How many wheels on a motorcycle?
Suppose there were 40 automobiles and 10 motorcycles at the show, how many wheels would that be?
Automobiles: $40 \times 4 = 160$
Motorcycles: $10 \times 2 = 20$
Total number of wheels = 180

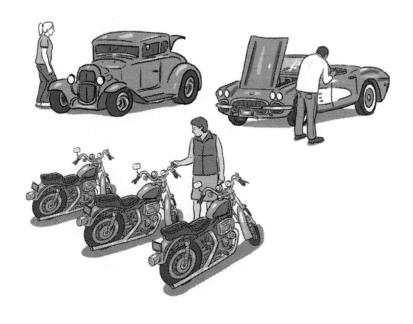

8 COUNTING AUTOMOBILES AND MOTORCYCLES

The Parnell family came back from a combined automobile-motorcycle show impressed by all the new models they saw. The brochure said that there were 70 different vehicles on display with a total of 200 wheels. How many were automobiles? How many were motorcycles?

SOLUTION

Suppose there were 30 automobiles and 10 motorcycles at the show, how many wheels would that be?

To compute the total number of wheels for the automobiles, multiply: $30 \times 4 = 120$.

To compute the total number of wheels for the motorcycles, multiply: $10 \times 2 = 20$.

So, the total number of wheels is $120 + 20 = 140$.

Keep trying. Make a table.

# of automobiles	# of motorcycles	# of vehicles	Total # of wheels
30	10	40	140
40	10	50	180
40	20	60	200
30	40	70	200

Answer: 30 automobiles and 40 motorcycles.

9 FINDING PENTOMINOES

Here are 5 identical squares that connect to each other along their edges.

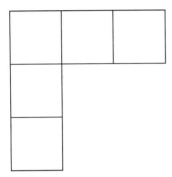

How many different arrangements of these squares are possible? Draw 6 other arrangements of 5 squares that connect along their sides.

HINTS

Ask students to arrange identical cardboard squares or floor tiles to make models of pentominoes.
Pentominoes means 5 squares joined together side by side.

9 FINDING PENTOMINOES

Here are 5 identical squares that connect to each other along their edges.

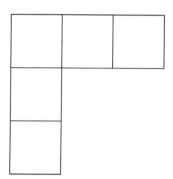

How many different arrangements of these squares are possible? Draw 6 other arrangements of 5 squares that connect along their sides.

SOLUTIONS

Answer: Here are the other 11 pentominoes. Find your drawings here.

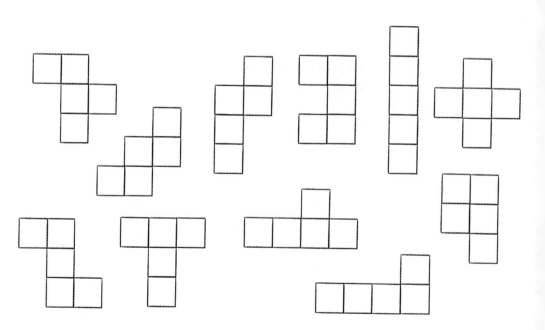

10 PAINTING A CUBE

This large cube is made up of 27 identical cubes. The dimensions of the larger cube are 3 small cubes long by 3 small cubes wide by 3 small cubes high.

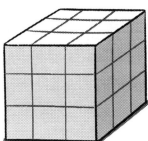

Suppose you paint the larger cube red on all its 6 faces.

Question 1: How many of the small cubes have all 6 faces painted?
Question 2: How many of the small cubes have 5 faces painted?
Question 3: How many of the small cubes have 4 faces painted?
Question 4: How many of the small cubes have 3 faces painted?
Question 5: How many of the small cubes have 2 faces painted?
Question 6: How many of the small cubes have 1 face painted?
Question 7: How many of the small cubes have no faces painted?

After you figure out the answers, the sum of all the answers should equal 27.

HINTS

Use a plastic or wooden model of a cube.
If possible, this model will show the smaller cubes.
Or, build a cube using 27 small identical cubes.
Answer to Question 1 above: none. Why?
Answer to Question 2 above: none. Why?
Answer to Question 3 above: none. Why?
Continue answering Questions 4, 5, 6, 7.

10 PAINTING A CUBE

This large cube is made up of 27 identical cubes. The dimensions of the larger cube are 3 small cubes long by 3 small cubes wide by 3 small cubes high.

Suppose you paint the larger cube red on all its 6 faces.

Question 1: How many of the small cubes have all 6 faces painted?
Question 2: How many of the small cubes have 5 faces painted?
Question 3: How many of the small cubes have 4 faces painted?
Question 4: How many of the small cubes have 3 faces painted?
Question 5: How many of the small cubes have 2 faces painted?
Question 6: How many of the small cubes have 1 face painted?
Question 7: How many of the small cubes have no faces painted?

After you figure out the answers, the sum of all the answers should equal 27.

SOLUTIONS

Answers:

Question 4: Where are the small cubes that have 3 faces painted? At the **8** vertices of the large cube.

Question 5: Where are the small cubes that have 2 faces painted? In the middle of the **12** edges of the large cube.

Question 6: Where are the small cubes that have 1 face painted? In the centers of the **6** faces of the large cube.

Question 7: Where are the small cubes that have no faces painted? There is only **1** cube that is not painted. You cannot see that cube as it is in the middle of the large cube.

Add all the small cubes that are painted: 8 + 12 + 6 + 1 = 27

11 GETTING IT RIGHT

```
  W R O N G
+ W R O N G
  R I G H T
```

Each letter stands for a different digit. The digits are 0, 1, 2, 3, 4, 5, 6, 7, 8, 9.

Find the correct digits standing for the letters.

W = _____   G = _____

R = _____   I = _____

O = _____   H = _____

N = _____   T = _____

HINTS

See the letters G and R? They are each 2 digits in the numbers added and 1 digit each in the sum.

The G in the sum is the same as the 2 Gs in the ones column.

The sum is 5 digits, so the sum of the 2 Ws is less than 10.

The digit W cannot be equal to 5, or greater than 5.

W must be 1, 2, 3, or 4.

Now go back to the ones column: G + G = T.

Try G = 4, so 4 + 4 = T. T = 8.

Try N = 3 in the tens column. So, H = 3 + 3 = 6.

O could be 2. 2 + 2 = 4.

We have G = 4, T = 8, N = 3, H = 6.

Try a different number for R.

11 GETTING IT RIGHT

```
  W R O N G
+ W R O N G
  R I G H T
```

Each letter stands for a different digit. The digits are 0, 1, 2, 3, 4, 5, 6, 7, 8, 9.

Find the correct digits standing for the letters.

W = ____   G = ____

R = ____   I = ____

O = ____   H = ____

N = ____   T = ____

SOLUTIONS

Start in the ones column: G + G = T.
Try G = 4, so 4 + 4 = T. T = 8.
Try N = 3 in the tens column. H = 3 + 3.
Do you see why O cannot be 2?
O has to be 7. 7 + 7 = 14.
R = 5, so I = 1, and W = 2.

Answer:

```
  25734
+ 25734
  51468
```

Are there any other solutions? Yes, here is one:

```
  49265
+ 49265
  98530
```

12 PASSING TRAINS

A train traveling from Metropolis (M) to Townsville (T) leaves every hour on the hour, 24 hours per day every day. The trip takes 12 hours.

Laura leaves on a train from T to M at 8 am traveling at the same speed as the train from M to T. She looks out of a window during the entire trip. How many trains from Metropolis to Townsville does she see on her journey? Explain your answer.

HINTS

How long does her trip take?
When will she arrive in Metropolis?
How <u>often</u> does Laura see a train?
Does she see the train that left at 8 pm the night before her trip?
Does she see the train that left at 9 pm the night before?

12 PASSING TRAINS

A train traveling from Metropolis (M) to Townsville (T) leaves every hour on the hour, 24 hours per day every day. The trip takes 12 hours.

Laura leaves on a train from T to M at 8 am traveling at the same speed as the train from M to T. She looks out of a window during the entire trip. How many trains from Metropolis to Townsville does she see on her journey? Explain your answer.

SOLUTION

Laura's trip takes 12 hours.

Laura will see these trains on her trip from T to M:

As she leaves at 8 am, she sees last night's 8 pm train from M to T arriving.

She also sees the 7 pm, 6 pm, 5 pm and so forth up to the 7 am train – **12 trains**.

But since she leaves on her trip at 8 am, she also sees the 8 am train to T that leaves at the same time as her train, and the 9 am train to T leaving 1 hour after she left T.

In addition to the 9 am train she also sees the 10 am, 11 am, 12 pm trains and so forth up to the 8 pm train, which she sees leaving as she arrives in M. That's another **13 trains**.

Answer: Total 25 trains.

13 TAKING THE CENSUS?

A robocall asks residents of Smithville about the number of people living in each home. It asks several questions. These are the questions and answers about children for one family.

Q: How many children live here?

A: Three. All girls.

Q: What are the ages of the children?

A: The product of their ages is 72.

Q: That is weird. Is any child older than 16?

A: No.

Q: Tell me more.

A: The sum of their ages is the address of this house.

Q: That is even weirder! I don't get it.

A: Why is that weirder? You know our address is 14 Mt. Osbourne Ct.

Q: Now I am beginning to get it! But...

A: Oh, the oldest child loves robots!

Q: (after a short pause) Now I have it! Thank you.

How old are the three children?

HINTS

"Product" means to multiply the three ages.
Let the ages be a, b, and c. So, $a \times b \times c = 72$.
And $a + b + c = 14$.
What are the ages a, b, and c?
Can they be 1, 2, and 36 since $1 \times 2 \times 36 = 72$?
No, since no child is older than 16.
Here are the possibilities:

3, 4, 6
1, 6, 12
2, 3, 12
1, 8, 9
2, 4, 9
3, 3, 8
2, 6, 6

13 TAKING THE CENSUS?

A robocall asks residents of Smithville about the number of people living in each home. It asks several questions. These are the questions and answers about children for one family.

Q: How many children live here?

A: Three. All girls.

Q: What are the ages of the children?

A: The product of their ages is 72.

Q: That is weird. Is any child older than 16?

A: No.

Q: Tell me more.

A: The sum of their ages is the address of this house.

Q: That is even weirder! I don't get it.

A: Why is that weirder? You know our address is 14 Mt. Osbourne Ct.

Q: Now I am beginning to get it! But...

A: Oh, the oldest child loves robots!

Q: (after a short pause) Now I have it! Thank you.

How old are the three children?

SOLUTIONS

Here are the possible ages of the three children:

3, 4, 6
1, 6, 12
2, 3, 12
1, 8, 9
2, 4, 9
3, 3, 8
2, 6, 6

The sum of their ages is 14.
Only 3, 3, 8 and 2, 6, 6 add to 14. Hmm.

Answer:

Remember: "Oh, the <u>oldest</u> child loves robots!"
So, the ages are 3, 3, 8, where there is an oldest child.

14 FINDING THE DAY OF BIRTH

Franz's 15th birthday is April 10, 2025. It is on Thursday. Find the day of the week Franz was born. Show how you figured this out.

HINTS

April 10, 2025 is a Thursday.
What is the day of the week a year before: April 10, 2024?
A year before means go back 365 days. That is 52 weeks and 1 day.
Go back exactly 52 weeks and you land on a Thursday.
Go back one more day. April 10, 2024 is a Wednesday.
April 10, 2025 is a Thursday.
April 10, 2024 is a Wednesday.
How many days do we go back from April 10, 2024 to April 10, 2023?
Go back 366 days because of the extra day in leap year 2024.
366 days is 52 weeks and 2 days. 52 weeks back gets us to Wednesday. Then 2 more days.
What day of the week is April 10, 2023? It is Monday.
Use these same ideas to go back 15 years.

14 FINDING THE DAY OF BIRTH

Franz's 15th birthday is April 10, 2025. It is on Thursday. Find the day of the week Franz was born. Show how you figured this out.

SOLUTIONS

Use the ideas of the hints.

Franz was born in 2010. Start in 2025 and go back 15 years.

Figure out the number of leap years from 2025 to 2010.

There are 4 leap years: 2024, 2020, 2016, and 2012. Each year back equals a day back, but leap year equals 2 days back.

Do the math: 15 years back for Franz: $11 \times 1 + 4 \times 2 = 19$ days back from Thursday. That is 2 weeks and 5 days back.

Answer: 2 weeks back = Thursday and back 5 more days = Saturday.

15 FOLDING SQUARES INTO OPEN CUBES

Do you see how this set of squares folds into a cube with an open top?

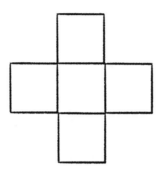

There are 8 sets of 5 squares that can fold into a cube with an open top. All squares touch other squares along their sides. (They are part of the full set of pentominoes – see Problem 9.)

Draw the other 7 sets of 5 squares that fold into a cube with an open top.

HINTS

Start by drawing different sets of 5 squares connected along their sides.

See Problem 9.

With each drawing, try to figure out if the squares fold to an open cube.

15 FOLDING SQUARES INTO OPEN CUBES

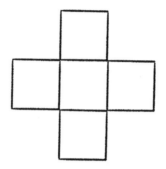

There are 8 sets of 5 squares that can fold into a cube with an open top. All squares touch other squares along their sides. (They are part of the full set of pentominoes – see Problem 9.)

Draw the other 7 sets of 5 squares that fold into a cube with an open top.

SOLUTIONS

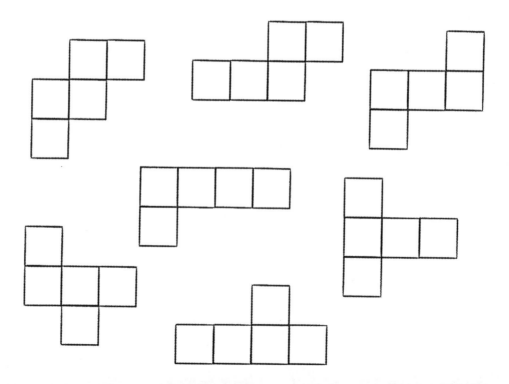

16 USING HANDSHAKES TO FIND HOW MANY

A teacher walks into her classroom. A student says to her: we all just shook hands with each other. We counted 105 handshakes. If every student shook the hand of every other student, how many students are in the classroom?

HINTS

This is really the so-called "handshakes problem" backwards.
Let's go back to counting handshakes:

How many students?	How many handshakes?
2	1
3	3
4	6
5	10
6	15
?	105

Find the pattern of handshakes.
Can you complete the chart to 105?

16 USING HANDSHAKES TO FIND HOW MANY

A teacher walks into her classroom. A student says to her: we all just shook hands with each other. We counted 105 handshakes. If every student shook the hand of every other student, how many students are in the classroom?

SOLUTIONS

Notice the pattern to the handshakes.
Subtract the numbers in the handshakes column.
The differences in handshakes increase by 1.
Write down the number of handshakes starting with 6 students and continuing until the number of handshakes totals 105.

Number of students	Number of handshakes
6	15
7	21
8	28
9	36
10	45
11	55
12	66
13	78
14	91
15	105

Answer: 105 handshakes result when 15 students shake hands with each other.

17 COUNTING TOOTHPICKS

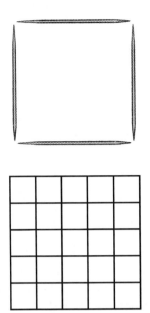

The grid is 5 toothpicks wide and 5 toothpicks long and contains 25 small squares. The length of each toothpick is equal to the sides of the small squares.

How many toothpicks do you need to form this 5 by 5 square grid?

HINTS

How many toothpicks make a 1 by 1 square?
How many toothpicks make a 2 by 2 square?
How many toothpicks make a 3 by 3 square?

Can you do it by counting carefully?

Do you see a pattern? Make a table.

17 COUNTING TOOTHPICKS

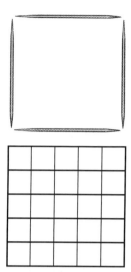

The grid is 5 toothpicks wide and 5 toothpicks long and contains 25 small squares. The length of each toothpick is equal to the sides of the small squares.

How many toothpicks do you need to form this 5 by 5 square grid?

SOLUTION 1: by counting

Count the number on the borders: 20
Count the number in the columns: 20
Count the number in the rows: 20

Answer: Total = 60 toothpicks

SOLUTION 2: by patterns

How many toothpicks make a 1 by 1 square? 4
How many toothpicks make a 2 by 2 square? 12
How many toothpicks make a 3 by 3 square? 24

Size of square	How many toothpicks?
1 by 1	4
2 by 2	12
3 by 3	24
4 by 4	40
5 by 5	

There is a pattern. The changes in the 2nd column are up by 8, up by 12, up by 16 – the increases go up by 4.

Answer: 5 by 5 will be up by 20: 40 + 20 = 60

18 GETTING HEADS AND TAILS

Ahuva tosses three quarters at the same time. What are all the results she could get?

List the results.

HINTS

Each coin will come up heads (H) or tails (T).
Is this possible: HHH?
How about this: TTT?
Write all possibilities with 2 Hs.
Then, write all possibilities with 2 Ts.
Are there more?

18 GETTING HEADS AND TAILS

Ahuva tosses three quarters at the same time. What are all the results she could get?

List the results.

SOLUTIONS

HHH	HHT	TTH
TTT	HTH	THT
	THH	HTT

Answer: There are 8 possible ways for 3 coins to land.

19 FINDING AREA ON A GRID

The area of each small square equals 1 square unit.

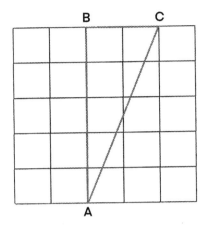

What is the area of triangle ABC (in square units)?

Explain how you got your answer.

HINT

The side AC of triangle ABC divides a rectangle in half.

19 FINDING AREA ON A GRID

The area of each small square equals 1 square unit.

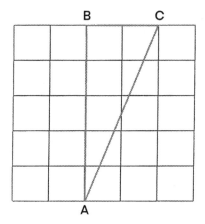

What is the area of triangle ABC (in square units)?

Explain how you got your answer.

SOLUTION

The side AC of triangle ABC divides a rectangle in half.
What is the area of the rectangle (area of each small square = 1)? 10

Answer: The area of triangle ABC is 5.

20 LINING UP PAILS

Here are six pails in a row. Three of the pails are filled with water and three are empty. Move only one pail to make the line of pails end in this alternating pattern: full, empty, full, empty, full, empty.

HINT

This is what you want at the end:

20 LINING UP PAILS

Here are six pails in a row. Three of the pails are filled with water and three are empty. Move only one pail to make the line of pails end in this alternating pattern: full, empty, full, empty, full, empty.

SOLUTION

The standard way of thinking would be **moving a pail** into a new position.
But maybe you can move **water** from one pail to another.

Pour water from the second pail into the fifth pail.
And you have:

21 FINDING PRIME NUMBERS

A prime number is a number that can be divided by only two numbers: 1 and itself.

Here are the prime numbers less than 50: 2, 3, 5, 7, 11, 13, 17, 19, 23, 29, 31, 37, 41, 43, 47.

2 is the only even prime. 1 is not a prime number because it can be divided by only one number.

If a number is not prime, it is called a composite number.

   1. Find all prime numbers between 50 and 100.

<u>Twin primes</u> are 2 prime numbers separated by 1 composite number. 11 and 13 are twin primes.

   2. Find a pair of twin primes between 50 and 100.

HINTS

Be careful. Is 51 a prime number?
Is 53?
Is 59?
Is 91?
What is the first pair of twin primes between 50 and 100?

21 FINDING PRIME NUMBERS

A prime number is a number that can be divided by only two numbers: 1 and itself.

Here are the prime numbers less than 50: 2, 3, 5, 7, 11, 13, 17, 19, 23, 29, 31, 37, 41, 43, 47.

2 is the only even prime. 1 is not a prime number because it can be divided by only one number.

If a number is not prime, it is called a composite number.

    1. Find all prime numbers between 50 and 100.

Twin primes are 2 prime numbers separated by 1 composite number. 11 and 13 are twin primes.

    2. Find a pair of twin primes between 50 and 100.

SOLUTIONS

Here are the prime numbers between 50 and 100: 53, 59, 61, 67, 71, 73, 79, 83, 89, 97 – ten in all.

Answer: There are two pairs of twin primes: 59 and 61; 71 and 73.

22 PAINTING A CUBE... AGAIN

Chenzi wants to paint each face of a cube completely in one color. What is the minimum number of colors she needs to make sure that no two adjacent faces have the same color?

HINTS

How many faces are there on a cube?
What does "adjacent" mean when we say adjacent faces?
Where are the faces that are not adjacent?

22 PAINTING A CUBE... AGAIN

Chenzi wants to paint each face of a cube completely in one color. What is the minimum number of colors she needs to make sure that no two adjacent faces have the same color?

SOLUTION

The faces that are not adjacent to each other are the faces opposite each other.

Opposite faces do not touch each other.

There are three pairs of opposite faces. Do you see them?

Answer: The minimum number of colors Chenzi can use is three.

23 DRAWING CAREFULLY

Here are small triangles inside a larger triangle.

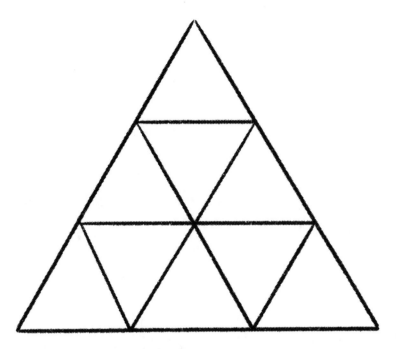

Is it possible to draw this figure without taking your pencil off the paper or crossing any lines?

HINTS

Experiment several times by using a pencil or a finger to trace over this figure to find a strategy.

23 DRAWING CAREFULLY

Here are small triangles inside a larger triangle.

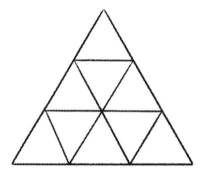

Is it possible to draw this figure without taking your pencil off the paper or crossing any lines?

SOLUTION

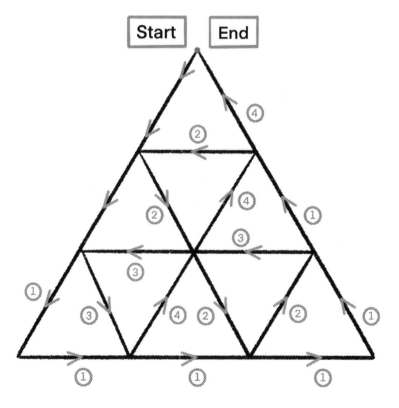

Are there any other solutions?

24 KEEPING IT REAL

Jared has nine coins that look the same. One of the coins is a counterfeit coin, slightly lighter than the rest. How can Jared find this lighter one by using a balance scale twice?

HINTS

All coins weigh the same, except one. That one is lighter than the rest.

Suppose you weighed 4 coins against 4 coins, and you found that the left side was lighter. What would you do next?

24 KEEPING IT REAL

Jared has nine coins that look the same. One of the coins is a counterfeit coin, slightly lighter than the rest. How can Jared find this lighter one by using a balance scale twice?

SOLUTIONS

Weigh 4 coins against 4 coins.
The left side of the scale dips, meaning the 4 coins on the left weigh less than the 4 coins on the right.
If you separate the lighter 4 coins into 2 and 2, one side will be lighter.
But you still do not know which coin is the lighter one of the 9 coins.

Answers: Weigh 3 against 3 coins on the scale.

If the scale balances, you know the lighter coin is among the remaining 3.

Weigh 1 against 1. If the scale balances, then the remaining coin is the lighter one. If the scale does not balance, take 2 of the 3 coins from the lighter side and weigh 1 against 1. If the scale balances, then the third coin is the lighter one.

25 FINDING N COINS EQUAL TO $1

You are using these coins to equal $1: half dollars, quarters, dimes, nickels, and pennies. Starting with the number 2, you realize that you can put 2 coins together to equal a dollar.

For 2 coins:
2 half dollars = $1
Then you try 3 coins:
1 half dollar + 2 quarters = $1
And 4 coins:
2 quarters + 2 quarters = $1
Keep going.
Here's 9 coins: 7 dimes + 1 nickel + 1 quarter = $1

1) Can you put together 20 coins to make $1?
2) Can you put together 25 coins to make $1?
3) Can you put together 30 coins to make $1?

HINTS

How do you put together 10 coins to equal $1?
10 dimes = $1
How many nickels make a dollar?

25 FINDING N COINS EQUAL TO $1

You are using these coins to equal $1: half dollars, quarters, dimes, nickels, and pennies. Starting with the number 2, you realize that you can put 2 coins together to equal a dollar.

For 2 coins:
2 half dollars = $1
Then you try 3 coins:
1 half dollar + 2 quarters = $1
And 4 coins:
2 quarters + 2 quarters = $1
Keep going.
Here's 9 coins: 7 dimes + 1 nickel + 1 quarter = $1

1) Can you put together 20 coins to make $1?
2) Can you put together 25 coins to make $1?
3) Can you put together 30 coins to make $1?

SOLUTIONS

1) For 20 coins: **20 nickels = $1**
2) For 25 coins: **3 dimes + 12 nickels + 10 pennies = 30c + 60c + 10c = $1**
3) For 30 coins: **2 quarters + 2 dimes + 1 nickel + 25 pennies = 50c + 20c + 5c + 25c = $1.**

Try It! More Math Problems for All
Photocopiable Problems

What follows are photocopiable versions of all 25 problems. These can be copied and used in group settings or used as handouts where access to a student workbook is unavailable.

DOI: 10.4324/9781003406587-2

1 FINDING A PAIR IN THE DARK

You have 10 red socks and 10 blue socks mixed in a drawer. These socks are all the same except for color. One night you enter the room in pitch darkness and open the drawer to get a pair of socks. What is the smallest number of socks you must pick out of the drawer to insure you have a pair of socks of the same color? Remember you cannot see what you picked.

2 PLANTING BUSHES IN A LINE

Ahmed wanted to make an attractive design from the 10 bushes he bought for the front lawn. He was able to plant the 10 identical bushes in 5 lines of 4 bushes each. How can that be done? Show it with a drawing.

3 DIVIDING LAND EQUALLY

Carmen owns a large tract of land in the shape of a square.

She wants to divide the land equally among her four sons. She first divides the land into four equal squares and takes one of the squares for herself. How can she divide the remaining land among her four sons, so each gets the same area and the same shape?

Draw your answer. Show the area Carmen keeps for herself and the shape of the areas she gives to her sons.

4 CHOOSING ONE FOR ALL

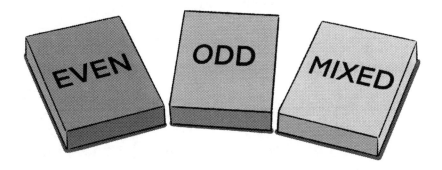

Your friend Wayne shows you three boxes of cards.

Box A: all cards have even numbers.

Box B: all cards have odd numbers.

Box C: cards are mixed – some have even numbers and the rest have odd numbers.

The three boxes have labels on top – EVEN, ODD, MIXED. But the labels are mixed up and not on the right boxes.

How can you choose one card from one box and tell exactly what is in all three boxes? Explain.

5 CONSTRUCTING REVOLUTIONARY EQUATIONS

Use each digit of 1776 once to construct equations. Here is an example equal to 3.

$$6 \div (1 + 7/7) = 3$$

Now use each digit of 1776 once to construct an equation equal to each of these digits: 1, 2, 4, 5, 6, 7, 8, 9.

That means write eight different equations.

_____ = 1		_____ = 6	
_____ = 2		_____ = 7	
_____ = 4		_____ = 8	
_____ = 5		_____ = 9	

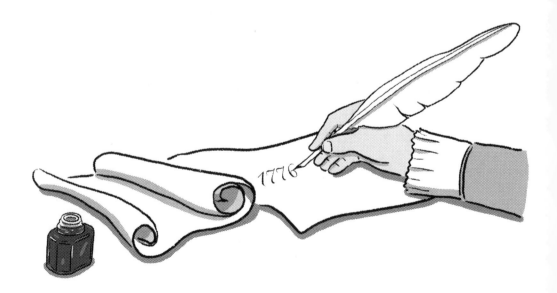

6 ARRIVING AT THE SAME TIME?

You have two clocks in front of you. Clock #1 runs smoothly.
Clock #2 also runs smoothly and at the same rate as Clock #1,
but the hands move backwards. If they both start at 8 o'clock,
when will they show the same time again? Explain.

7 GETTING TO 50 FIRST

Let's play the Game of 50. You and a friend both start at 0 along the same number line.

Decide who goes first and then take turns. For every turn, players advance by at least one step, but no more than six steps. When it is your turn, say the number of steps you will take. The first person to get to 50 wins.

Figure out a winning strategy.

8 COUNTING AUTOMOBILES AND MOTORCYCLES

The Parnell family came back from a combined automobile-motorcycle show impressed by all the new models they saw. The brochure said that there were 70 different vehicles on display with a total of 200 wheels. How many were automobiles? How many were motorcycles?

9 FINDING PENTOMINOES

Here are 5 identical squares that connect to each other along their edges.

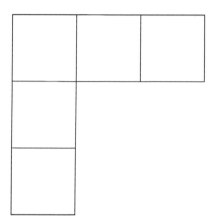

How many different arrangements of these squares are possible? Draw 6 other arrangements of 5 squares that connect along their sides.

10 PAINTING A CUBE

This large cube is made up of 27 identical cubes. The dimensions of the larger cube are 3 small cubes long by 3 small cubes wide by 3 small cubes high.

Suppose you paint the larger cube red on all its 6 faces.

Question 1: How many of the small cubes have all 6 faces painted?

Question 2: How many of the small cubes have 5 faces painted?

Question 3: How many of the small cubes have 4 faces painted?

Question 4: How many of the small cubes have 3 faces painted?

Question 5: How many of the small cubes have 2 faces painted?

Question 6: How many of the small cubes have 1 face painted?

Question 7: How many of the small cubes have no faces painted?

After you figure out the answers, the sum of all the answers should equal 27.

11 GETTING IT RIGHT

```
  W R O N G
+ W R O N G
  R I G H T
```

Each letter stands for a different digit. The digits are 0, 1, 2, 3, 4, 5, 6, 7, 8, 9.

Find the correct digits standing for the letters.

W = _____   G = _____
R = _____   I = _____
O = _____   H = _____
N = _____   T = _____

12 PASSING TRAINS

A train traveling from Metropolis (M) to Townsville (T) leaves every hour on the hour, 24 hours per day every day. The trip takes 12 hours.

Laura leaves on a train from T to M at 8 am traveling at the same speed as the train from M to T. She looks out of a window during the entire trip. How many trains from Metropolis to Townsville does she see on her journey? Explain your answer.

13 TAKING THE CENSUS?

A robocall asks residents of Smithville about the number of people living in each home. It asks several questions. These are the questions and answers about children for one family.

Q: How many children live here?

A: Three. All girls.

Q: What are the ages of the children?

A: The product of their ages is 72.

Q: That is weird. Is any child older than 16?

A: No.

Q: Tell me more.

A: The sum of their ages is the address of this house.

Q: That is even weirder! I don't get it.

A: Why is that weirder? You know our address is 14 Mt. Osbourne Ct.

Q: Now I am beginning to get it! But…

A: Oh, the oldest child loves robots!

Q: (after a short pause) Now I have it! Thank you.

How old are the three children?

14 FINDING THE DAY OF BIRTH

Franz's 15th birthday is April 10, 2025. It is on a Thursday. Find the day of the week Franz was born. Show how you figured this out.

15 FOLDING SQUARES INTO OPEN CUBES

Do you see how this set of squares folds into a cube with an open top?

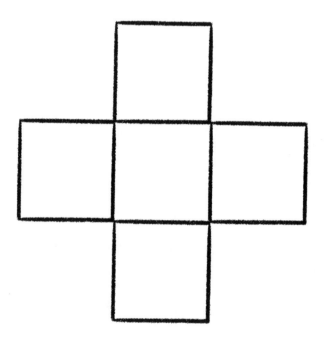

There are 8 sets of 5 squares that can fold into a cube with an open top. All squares touch other squares along their sides. (They are part of the full set of pentominoes – see Problem 9.)

Draw the other 7 sets of 5 squares that fold into a cube with an open top.

16 USING HANDSHAKES TO FIND HOW MANY

A teacher walks into her classroom. A student says to her: we all just shook hands with each other. We counted 105 handshakes. If every student shook the hand of every other student, how many students are in the classroom?

17 COUNTING TOOTHPICKS

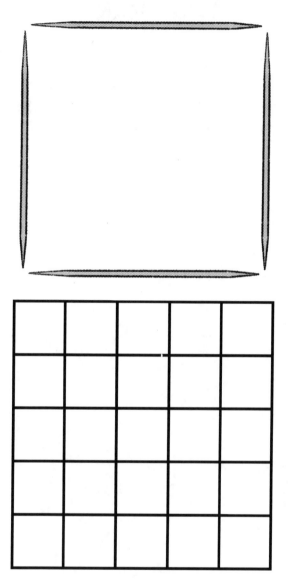

The grid is 5 toothpicks wide and 5 toothpicks long and contains 25 small squares. The length of each toothpick is equal to the sides of the small squares.

How many toothpicks do you need to form this 5 by 5 square grid?

18 GETTING HEADS AND TAILS

Ahuva tosses three quarters at the same time. What are all the results she could get?

List the results.

19 FINDING AREA ON A GRID

The area of each small square equals 1 square unit.

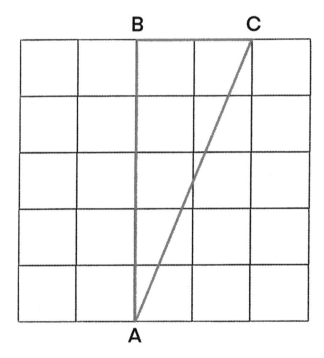

What is the area of triangle ABC (in square units)?

Explain how you got your answer.

20 LINING UP PAILS

Here are six pails in a row. Three of the pails are filled with water and three are empty. Move only one pail to make the line of pails end in this alternating pattern: full, empty, full, empty, full, empty.

21 FINDING PRIME NUMBERS

A prime number is a number that can be divided by only two numbers: 1 and itself.

Here are the prime numbers less than 50: 2, 3, 5, 7, 11, 13, 17, 19, 23, 29, 31, 37, 41, 43, 47.

2 is the only even prime. 1 is not a prime number because it can be divided by only one number.

If a number is not prime, it is called a composite number.

   1. Find all prime numbers between 50 and 100.

<u>Twin primes</u> are 2 prime numbers separated by 1 composite number. 11 and 13 are twin primes.

   2. Find a pair of twin primes between 50 and 100.

22 PAINTING A CUBE... AGAIN

Chenzi wants to paint each face of a cube completely in one color. What is the minimum number of colors she needs to make sure that no two adjacent faces have the same color?

23 DRAWING CAREFULLY

Here are small triangles inside a larger triangle.

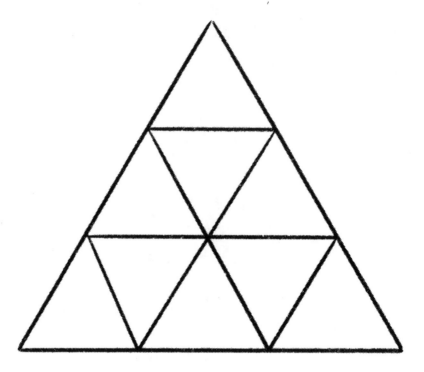

Is it possible to draw this figure without taking your pencil off the paper or crossing any lines?

24 KEEPING IT REAL

Jared has nine coins that look the same. One of the coins is a counterfeit coin, slightly lighter than the rest. How can Jared find this lighter one by using a balance scale twice?

25 FINDING N COINS EQUAL TO $1

You are using these coins to equal $1: half dollars, quarters, dimes, nickels, and pennies. Starting with the number 2, you realize that you can put 2 coins together to equal a dollar.

For 2 coins:
2 half dollars = $1
Then you try 3 coins:
1 half dollar + 2 quarters = $1
And 4 coins:
2 quarters + 2 quarters = $1
Keep going.
Here's 9 coins: 7 dimes + 1 nickel + 1 quarter = $1

1) Can you put together 20 coins to make $1?
2) Can you put together 25 coins to make $1?
3) Can you put together 30 coins to make $1?

About the Author

Dr. Kaplan is Professor Emeritus of Mathematics Education at Seton Hall University. Previously, he taught first grade and high school in New York City. Later, Jerry was Associate Professor at Teachers College, Columbia University, and Visiting Professor at the University of Tel Aviv, Israel. He has conducted research and written widely on many areas of teaching and learning mathematics, applying research to the practical needs of the mathematics curriculum and classroom.

Among his many interests in education, one stands out – the role of problem solving activities that combine more than one area of the school's curriculum. Call it cross-curriculum problem solving. In spite of the efforts of Jerry and others, he admits that this area has not caught on, but thinks the time is now ripe for problem solving.

Jerry designed and wrote special books for **Triumph Learning** to help students prepare for state and national tests. These books, all bearing the title "**Coach**", are tailored to students who have difficulty with math and math tests.

He has led many workshops, seminars, and classes on how to implement problem solving into new curricula. He always encourages teachers to reach beyond the ordinary to include problem solving and non-standard experiences for their students.

Several beneficiaries of his work in these areas have been the Job Corps Program, the Ford Foundation, the Educational Testing Service, and the Ministry of Education, Israel.

He is a co-author of a set of books for McGraw-Hill, a major textbook series for Harcourt School Publishers, high school texts for SRA, and a management learning system for Random House.

About the Illustrator

Ysemay Dercon is a freelance illustrator and graduate of the Rhode Island School of Design. She is currently based in Providence, Rhode Island. Her creative pursuits lie in the worlds of publishing, art and science communication, portraiture, and journalistic illustration. She strives to create art that communicates about the world around us in a meaningful and engaging way. You can find her work in books such as *The Little Gardener. Helping Children Connect with the Natural World*, a primer on gardening meant for both children and adults, published by Princeton Architectural Press. She has also worked closely with Osa Conservation, a non-profit conservation and research organization located in the Osa Peninsula of Costa Rica. Her collaboration with Osa Conservation involved creating the illustrations for a series of interpretive panels that have been installed on the trail system of the organization's property. When not creating, she enjoys going for long walks outdoors, reading memoirs, and spending time in cafes with friends.

Printed in the United States
by Baker & Taylor Publisher Services